Vocabulary and Spelling
Practice Book

ISBN: 0-13-437579-3

1 2 3 4 5 6 7 8 9 10   03 02 01 00 99

Prentice Hall
Upper Saddle River, New Jersey
Glenview, Illinois
Needham, Massachusetts

Contents

To the Student

This book is divided into two parts, **Vocabulary Development** and **Spelling Applications.** Each section provides practice pages to help you improve your vocabulary and spelling skills. The vocabulary practice focuses on eleventh grade vocabulary and the vocabulary you will be tested on when you take the SATs. The spelling practice highlights spelling rules and words that are exceptions to the rules, words often misused in writing, and words considered difficult to spell for many people. The activities allow you to use a dictionary or thesaurus when necessary.

The vocabulary practice pages will increase your knowledge of prefixes, suffixes, and word roots to help you understand new words in your reading. Studying synonyms, antonyms, connotations, and denotations will help you determine the meanings of unfamiliar words when you are reading. Learning the differences between words that sound like other words will help you to use them correctly in writing and speaking and help you to recognize the differences when you are reading.

In vocabulary practice, you will write definitions of words, write sentences using new vocabulary, form words by combining word parts, identify the correct choice of words in text, complete sentences and passages with new vocabulary, and identify the connotations of words in context. You will also learn to identify and complete several types of analogies.

The spelling practice pages will improve your ability to spell with accuracy, an important skill for writing. You will apply spelling rules to correct misspelled words, learn the differences between words with similar spellings and meanings, and learn to spell those words that are commonly misspelled by many people—words sometimes called "spelling demons."

Good spellers use the following guidelines to improve their spelling skills.
1. Learn the pronunciation of a word.
2. Learn the word origin or root.
3. Learn the spelling rules and their exceptions.
4. Learn to spell words in small parts or syllables.
5. Picture a word by closing your eyes and spelling it.
6. Write the word often and use it in conversation.
7. Keep a list of difficult words. As you learn them, cross them off your list!

Remember that practice increases your vocabulary and your accuracy in spelling. Make your goal to improve your vocabulary and spelling skills to be a better reader, writer, and speaker. You will have a greater word knowledge and achieve higher test scores!

Vocabulary Practice 1: Prefixes

Prefixes: *e-, ef-, ex-*

A **prefix** is a word part added to the beginning of a word that changes the meaning of the word. Latin and Greek words with prefixes have changed spelling over time.

> **Example:** The Latin prefix *ef-* (also *ex-*) means "something external or outwardly directed." The Latin root *fundere,* means "to pour." This word is now *effusive,* which means "pouring freely" or "very enthusiastic." Other prefixes have meanings similar to *ef.* The prefix *e-* means "out" or "away from" and *ex-* means "taking or removing out of something."

A. Use the prefix, word origin, and sentence to write a definition for the boldface word. Check your definitions in a dictionary.

1. *expurgate* is *ex-* and *purgate* (from *purgare* meaning "to purge, purify")

   The office staff **expurgated** all the files when they moved to new headquarters.

   _____

2. *exonerate* is *ex-* and *onerate* (from *onerare* meaning "to load" or "to burden")

   After many years, costly investigations, and trials, the accused was **exonerated.**

   _____

3. *extricate* is *ex-* and *tricate* (from *tricae* meaning "obstacles or trivialities")

   The story protagonist was unable to **extricate** herself from her enemies' plots.

   _____

4. *effervescent* is *ef-* and *fervescent* (from *fervere* meaning "to boil")

   Jill was attractive and **effervescent**— always surrounded by admiring friends.

   _____

5. *emanate* is *e-* and *manate* (from *manare* meaning "to flow")

   Richard's expansive vocabulary **emanated** in lively and interesting conversation.

   _____

B. On another piece of paper, identify the origins and meanings of these prefixed words. Then, write their definitions and use the words in sentences.

1. efface _____

2. elapse _____

3. expatriate _____

4. elude _____

5. emit _____

   _____

   _____

   _____

   _____

Vocabulary Practice 2: Prefixes

Prefixes: *di-, dia-, dis-*

A **prefix** is a word part added to the beginning of a word that changes the meaning of the word. Latin and Greek words with prefixes have changed spelling over time.

Example: The Greek prefixes *dia-* and *dis-* are forms of the prefix *di-*. The prefix *dia-* means "through, apart, between," while *dis-* means "away, apart." The prefix *dis-* becomes *di-* before consonants *b, d, g, l, m, n, r,* or *v*.

A. Write the prefix *dis-* with the word to make the new word that matches the definition. Use a dictionary to check your answers.

approbation	cord	engage	integrate	avow
allow	enchanted	passionate	oblige	closure

	Prefix and Word	**Definition**
1.	_____	to deny knowledge or approval of
2.	_____	to refuse to do a favor for; to offend
3.	_____	unemotional, calm, composed
4.	_____	disapproval
5.	_____	lack of agreement; confused noise
6.	_____	to untangle or detach
7.	_____	to refuse to allow; to reject
8.	_____	set free from illusion
9.	_____	to separate into parts or fragments
10.	_____	something revealed or uncovered

B. Write five of the words you created in Exercise A to complete these sentences. Some words require suffixes.

1. Carl _____ the puppy's tether from the fence post so that he could run.

2. The association decided to _____ one proposal after a debate.

3. Visitors were _____ when they ran out of currency and asked for help.

4. When the teacher asked the child who was responsible, he _____ the situation.

5. A leader is demonstrative about issues, not _____ and unconcerned.

C. On another piece of paper, make a chart with the headings as shown below. Use the dictionary to get information about these words: *dichotomy, digress, dialect, diagnosis, diathermy, disparate, disconsolate, dispensation, discursive, disparagement.*

Word Prefix and Word Origin	**Definition**

Vocabulary Practice 3: Prefixes

Prefixes: *ab-, ob-*

A **prefix** is a word part added to the beginning of a word that changes the meaning of the word. Latin and Greek words with prefixes have changed spelling over time.

Example: The Latin prefix *ob-*, means "in the way" or "against." The Latin root *obstare*, means "to stand." This word is now *obstacle*, which means "that which opposes or stands in the way." The prefix *ab-*, similar to *ob-*, means "away" or "from," as in *abstain*, which means "to hold oneself away from or back."

A. Use the prefix, word origin, and sentence to write a definition for the boldface word. Check your definitions in a dictionary.

1. *aberration* is *ab-* and *erration* (from *errare* meaning "to wander, go astray")

   The new lab results were an **aberration** of the standard results recorded for the test.

   _____

2. *abstinence* is *ab-* and *tinence* (from *tenare* meaning "to hold.")

   Jim's new health plan included complete **abstinence** from junk food and candy.

   _____

3. *abstruse* is *ab-* and *truse* (from *trudere* meaning "to thrust or push.")

   The freshmen found the professor's new and confusing ideas quite **abstruse.**

   _____

4. *obviate* is *ob-* and *viate* (from *viam* meaning "way.")

   Carl thought that backup files would **obviate** the need for printing hard copies.

   _____

5. *obsequious* is *ob-* and *sequious* (from *sequi* meaning "to follow.")

   Charlotte's **obsequious** co-worker never disagreed with her.

   _____

B. Identify the origins and meanings of these prefixed words. Then, use the words in sentences.

1. abeyance _____

2. abhorrence _____

3. obdurate _____

4. abstract _____

5. obsess _____

_____

_____

_____

_____

_____

Vocabulary Practice 4: Prefixes

Prefixes: *co-, con-, com-, col-, cor-*

A **prefix** is a word part that is added to the beginning of a word that changes the meaning of the word.

> **Example:** The Latin prefix *co-* means "with" or "together." Adding *co-* to the word *operate*, meaning "to work," makes *cooperate*, which means "to work with" or "to work together." The prefixes *con-, com-, col-*, and *cor-* also mean "with" or "together."

A. Add a word to each prefix to make the new word that matches the definition.

trite	respond	glomerate	league	passionate
mensurable	**efficient**	**lateral**	**relate**	**ordinate**

1. *co* and _____ means "equal in importance, rank, or degree"

2. *col* and _____ means "running side by side; parallel"

3. *cor* and _____ means "to be in agreement or harmony"

4. *cor* and _____ means "to put into complementary or reciprocal relation"

5. *con* and _____ means "to form into an adhering or rounding mass"

6. *com* and _____ means "feeling or showing sympathy"

7. *col* and _____ means "a fellow member of a profession"

8. *con* and _____ means "feeling regret for one's offenses"

9. *co* and _____ means "a number or symbol multiplying a variable"

10. *com* and _____ means "measurable by a common standard"

B. Add *co-, con-, com-, col-*, or *cor-* to these words and write the new words. Then, write the words in the sentences.

mission _____ fluent _____ strict _____

incidence _____ lapse _____

1. Two _____ rivers created a huge delta at the mouth.

2. The gymnast was near _____ from exhaustion.

3. Jen didn't think it was a _____ that Julie wore an identical dress to the prom.

4. Last year's shoes were so small that Marco feared they would _____ his feet.

5. Tatiana hoped that the ad agency would _____ her to develop new art ideas.

C. Using a dictionary, make a list of other words with the prefixes *co-, con-, com-, col-*, or *cor-*.

Vocabulary Practice 5: Suffixes

Suffixes: *-ity, -ty, -y*

A **suffix** is a word part added to the end of a word that changes the word's meaning.

Example: The Latin suffixes *-ity, -ty,* and *-y,* mean "state or quality of." Adding *-ity* to *pure* makes *purity;* adding *-ty* to *loyal* makes *loyalty;* adding *y* to *fruit* makes *fruity.*

A. Underline the words in the sentences with the suffixes *-ity, -ty,* or *-y.* Then, write the letter of the definition before the sentence.

a. recklessness

b. government pardon

c. moral corruption

d. inadequate

e. lightness of manner or speech

f. something beyond doubt; a certainty

g. proud in a condescending way

h. daring; boldness

i. meaningful and brief

j. lacking in strictness or firmness

____ 1. The library offered amnesty to borrowers who returned overdue books.

____ 2. Brian's jokes added a touch of levity to the birthday celebration.

____ 3. Illegal campaign contributions added depravity to the governor's race.

____ 4. The principal criticized Mr. Banks for his laxity in classroom management.

____ 5. Jose thought the batter had audacity to argue over a called strike.

____ 6. The column on affordable day care was precise and pithy according to readers.

____ 7. Patty felt confident that her selection for the lead in *Our Town* was a surety.

____ 8. The guide scolded Jim for his temerity in hiking without proper equipment.

____ 9. Dena thought the cafeteria lunch portions were measured and scanty.

____ 10. The new senior class president walked with a vain and haughty air.

B. Write five more words with the suffixes *-ity, -ty,* and *-y* and define them on the lines below. Check your answers in a dictionary.

-ity	*-ty*	*-y*
_____	_____	_____
_____	_____	_____
_____	_____	_____
_____	_____	_____
_____	_____	_____
_____	_____	_____
_____	_____	_____
_____	_____	_____
_____	_____	_____
_____	_____	_____

Vocabulary Practice 6: Suffixes

Suffixes: *-ance, -ancy, -ence, -ency*

A **suffix** is a word part added to the end of a word that changes the word's meaning. Words have evolved from their origins in spelling and meaning over time.

Example: The Latin suffix *–ance* means "the act or process of" as in *acceptance,* or "the state or quality of " as in *appearance.* Other suffixes have spellings and meanings similar to *–ance.* The suffix *-ancy* is a form of *-ance* and has the same meaning. The suffix *-ence* means "act, fact, quality, state, result, or degree" and *-ency* is a form of *-ence* and has the same meaning.

A. Write the words with the suffixes listed to form new words. Some words change spellings when adding the suffix. Use a dictionary, if necessary.

-ance	*-ancy*	*-ence*	*-ency*
comply	tenant	indolent	expedient
vigil	occupy	eloquent	consistent
sustain	buoyant	defer	resilient
acquaint	vacant	creed	complacent
concord	hesitate	prude	insolvent
tolerate	discrepant	permanent	reside

New Words

_____ _____ _____ _____

_____ _____ _____ _____

_____ _____ _____ _____

_____ _____ _____ _____

_____ _____ _____ _____

_____ _____ _____ _____

B. Write ten words you wrote in Exercise A with their definitions.

Word   **Definition**

1. _____ a. ability to spring back into shape

2. _____ b. belief in another's report

3. _____ c. lack of agreement

4. _____ d. suitability for a given purpose

5. _____ e. that which maintains life

6. _____ f. a taking or keeping in possession

7. _____ g. careful management

8. _____ h. harmony

9. _____ i. bankruptcy

10. _____ j. dislike of work; idleness

C. On another piece of paper, write the definitions of the words you did *not* use in Exercise B.

Vocabulary Practice 7: Suffixes

Suffixes: -ary, -ery, -ry

A **suffix** is a word part added to the end of a word that changes the word's meaning. Words have evolved from their origins in spelling and meaning over time.

Example: The English word *literary*, which means "having the nature of literature," comes from the Latin word *littera*, meaning "letter." The suffix ending -ary means "having the nature of" or "concerning." Other suffixes with meanings similar to –ary are -ery and –ry, which mean "state or quality of."

A. Underline the words with the suffixes -ary, -ery, or -ry. Then select the definition for each underlined word and write the letter of the definition before the sentence.

a. boldness, shamelessness

b. inn, hotel

c. merrymaking

d. fixed, not movable

e. as an honor, without service or pay

f. living in the same period

g. a famous intellectual

h. figures of speech, descriptions

i. third in rank or order

j. unusual, exceptional

____ 1. Graduating students participated in celebrations and revelry until dawn.

____ 2. Whittier was a contemporary of Lowell and the other Fireside Poets.

____ 3. The teacher discussed the poem's imagery to create vivid pictures.

____ 4. People were surprised by the writer's effrontery at the interview.

____ 5. Jonas Salk was a luminary in the field of medicine.

____ 6. On our European vacation, we stayed at a very nice hostelry.

____ 7. Well-known philanthropists were given honorary degrees by the college.

____ 8. A woman held the tertiary position as second vice president.

____ 9. Long ago, school desks were stationary—a sign of the rigidity of classrooms.

____ 10. Through extraordinary efforts, police and dogs rescued a child in a fire.

B. Write two other words with the suffixes -ary, -ery, or -ry and use the words in sentences. Check your answers in a dictionary.

-ary	**-ery**	**-ry**
_____	_____	_____
_____	_____	_____
_____	_____	_____
_____	_____	_____
_____	_____	_____
_____	_____	_____
_____	_____	_____
_____	_____	_____

Vocabulary Practice 8: Suffixes

Suffixes: *-al, -etic, -ic, -ical*

A **suffix** is a word part added to the end of a word that changes the word's meaning. Words have evolved from their origins in meaning and spelling over time.

Example: The Greek suffix *-ic* means "relating to." Adding *-ic* to *poet* makes *poetic*, which means "characteristic of poetry." The suffixes *-etic, -ical,* and *-al* also mean "of" or "relating to."

A. Underline the suffixes *-ic, -etic, -ical,* or *-al* in the boldface words. Then, write a word from the list in each sentence.

ascetic "of self-discipline"; "denial"	**prolific** "producing abundance"
vitriolic "bitter and scathing"	**esoteric** "understood by a chosen few"
prosaic "straightforward"; "dull"	**banal** "drearily commonplace"; "trite"
polemical "of controversy or argument"	**euphonic** "agreeable to the ear"
soporific "causing sleep"; "lethargic"	**pedantic** "concern for rules"; "details"

1. The author, who produced two books a year, was a _____ writer.

2. Dr. Toth's new theory proved to be quite _____ at the recent science symposium.

3. When the teacher turned the lights off, the class found the film very _____.

4. The internal rhyme of the poem made it _____ when read aloud.

5. Bare walls and plain furniture made Trina's dorm room look _____.

6. The _____ article was readable only to those who understood baseball statistics.

7. A well-known columnist wrote a _____ critique of the pop star's new album.

8. With its theme of boy meets girl, the book was _____ and had no depth.

9. Hal wrote a very _____ essay, using no literary techniques or poetic styles.

10. Joy's _____ English professor spent more time on rules than on literature.

B. Write the word that is combined with the suffix to make the new word. Then, write the definition of the new word. Check your definitions in a dictionary.

academia	frenzy	botany	crypt	remedy

1. _____ and *-al* make *remedial* _____

2. _____ and *-ic* make *cryptic* _____

3. _____ and *-etic* make *frenetic* _____

4. _____ and *-ical* make *botanical* _____

5. _____ and *-ic* make *academic* _____

C. Write a sentence using each italicized word in Exercise B.

Vocabulary Practice 9: Word Roots

Word roots: *-fac-, -fact-, -fect-, -fic-*

A **word root** is a word part, or group of letters, that forms the basic part of a word and gives the word its primary meaning. Prefixes and suffixes add specific meanings to word roots. If you know the meaning of a word root, you can determine the meanings of the whole word.

Example: The Latin word *afficere* means "a state of feeling." The Latin root *-fect-* means "to do" or "to make." Adding the prefix *af-*, meaning "to" or "toward," and the suffix *-ion*, meaning "state or quality of," makes *affection*, which means "fondness" or "regard toward someone or something." The roots *-fac-*, *-fact-*, and *-fic-* also mean "to do or make."

A. Underline the root in each boldface word. Explain the meaning of the word as it is used in the phrase. Then, write a sentence using the phrase given or one of your own.

Example: effi<u>ci</u>ency expert *-fic-* A person who is knowledgeable about ways to produce something without waste of time, effort, money, and so forth.

The company hired an efficiency expert to help people save time.

1. course **proficiency** _____

_____

2. **defective** computer _____

_____

3. delicious **confection** _____

_____

4. **officious** maitre d' _____

_____

5. **facsimile** quality _____

_____

6. **infectious** laugh _____

_____

7. vocal **faction** _____

_____

8. **factual** article _____

_____

9. **fictitious** account _____

_____

10. diverse **faculty** _____

_____

B. On another piece of paper, write sentences for these words: *artifice, facile, efficient, fictional, refectory.*

Vocabulary Practice 10: Word Roots

Word roots: -ang-, -flect-, -flex-, -frag-, -fract-

A **word root** is a word part, or group of letters, that forms the basic part of a word and gives the word its primary meaning. If you know the meaning of a word root, you can determine the meaning of the whole word.

Example: The Latin root -flect- means "bend." Adding the prefix re-, meaning "back," and the suffix -ion, meaning "the state or quality of," to the root -flect- makes reflection, which means "a turning or bending back on oneself." Other roots have meanings similar to -flect-. The word roots -fract- and -frag- mean "break" and -flex- and -ang- mean "bend."

A. Choose and write the word that completes each sentence. Underline the roots in the answer choices.

1. A good driver is aware of other drivers' responses and has good _____.

   fragility   **reflexes**   **angles**

2. Dr. Newman has a(n) _____ schedule which allows him to see patients in an emergency.

   flexible   **angular**   **fragile**

3. The player _____ the ball with his hand, which saved him from injury.

   inflection   **refracted**   **deflected**

4. It was a(n) _____ of the law to make a U-turn, which the driver soon learned.

   fragment   **infraction**   **reflection**

5. The architect drew a(n) _____ window for the small corner space in the room.

   reflex   **flexible**   **angular**

6. Being _____ makes it difficult to change plans or be spontaneous.

   inflexible   **flexion**   **reflexive**

7. A kitten, found in the basement, was frightened, hungry, and in a _____ condition.

   fragmented   **refracted**   **fragile**

8. The _____ in Annabel's tone of voice revealed a question in her mind.

   fragility   **inflection**   **infraction**

9. Dr. Geuss examined and measured the _____ in his patient's leg .

   flexion   **refraction**   **reflection**

10. Many employees have _____ to accommodate their needs for family time.

    flexors   **angularity**   **flextime**

B. On another piece of paper, explain each answer in Exercise A in a statement like this:

   The word _____ is the answer because the root _____ means "_____" and the word _____ means "_____."

Then, choose five other words with the roots -ang-, -flect-, -flex-, -frag-, and -fract-, and write sentences using the words.

          © Prentice-Hall, Inc.

Vocabulary Practice 11: Word Roots

Word root: -ject-

A **word root** is a word part, or group of letters, that forms the basic part of a word and gives the word its primary meaning. Knowing the meaning of a word root can help you determine the meaning of the whole word.

> **Example:** The Latin root -ject- means "throw." Adding the prefix tra-, a form of trans-, meaning "across," and the suffix -ory, meaning "having the quality of," to the root -ject- makes trajectory, which means "the path of a moving body through space."

A. Add the prefixes to the root -ject- and write the new words in the first box. Then, add suffixes to the prefixed words you wrote and write those words in the second box. Write as many words as you think there are with the root -ject-. Write on another piece of paper, if necessary. Then, check all your words in a dictionary.

Prefix	Prefix Added to -ject-	Suffixes	Words with Prefixes and Suffixes
pro- "forward"	1. _____	**-ile** "suitable for"	1. _____
sub- "under"	2. _____	**-ion** "act or condition of"	2. _____
ob- "over, against, toward"	3. _____	**-ure** "action or process"	3. _____
re- "back, again"	4. _____	**-ive** "of, relating to"	4. _____
in- "into"	5. _____	**-or** "one who is or does"	5. _____
inter- "between, among"	6. _____		6. _____
de- "off, away from, down"	7. _____		7. _____
con- "with, together"	8. _____		8. _____
ab- "from, away"	9. _____		9. _____
e- "from, out"	10. _____		10. _____

B. Write the words from Exercise A in the sentences. You will use words from both columns.

1. The actor needed to learn how to _____ his voice to the back of the theater.

2. Diana decided to _____ her employer's contract proposal.

3. The predictions for the winner of the World Cup were all _____, or based on speculation.

4. The prosecutor knew that the defense would _____ to his questioning.

5. Some people believe that taste in art is purely _____ because it is so personal.

6. The vaccine was prescribed in the form of an _____ rather than orally.

7. Everyone felt complete _____ after losing to the worst team.

8. If the referee caught Larry in one more foul, he would _____ him from the game.

9. Mayors touring the country were disturbed by such _____ poverty.

10. A _____ hit the car from an explosion five hundred yards away.

Vocabulary Practice 12: Word Roots

Word roots: *-cap-, -capt-, -cept-, -cip-*

A **word root** is a word part, or group of letters, that forms the basic part of a word and gives the word its primary meaning. Knowing the meaning of a root can help you determine the meaning of the whole word.

> **Example:** The Latin root *-cip-* means "to take or receive." The Latin word *recipere* is now the English word *recipient,* which means "one who receives." Other roots have meanings similar to *-cip-*. The word root *-cept-* means "to take or receive" and *-cap-* and *-capt-* mean "to seize or hold."

A. Write the word that completes each sentence. Underline the root in each answer choice.

1. Colby's teacher handed back his incomplete paper, noting that it was _____.
   recaptured   **receptive**   **unacceptable**

2. Dana threw her candy wrapper into the nearest trash _____.
   receptacle   **reception**   **conception**

3. Lee assured her boss that she could _____ the project and begin work on it soon.
   recapitulate   **conceptualize**   **except**

4. The sophomores knew that to get "A's," their papers had to be _____.
   intercepted   **exceptional**   **participants**

5. Only a singer with Beth's star quality could _____ an audience so completely.
   capitalize   **capsize**   **captivate**

6. What _____ Susan's asthma attack was a mystery to Dr. Ross.
   precipitated   **reciprocated**   **recaptured**

7. Ben was known to be _____: he often saw through appearances to the truth.
   recipient   **percipient**   **reciprocal**

8. Deb was glad she had brought her camera to _____ the historic event.
   capitalize   **caption**   **capture**

9. The _____ newspaper ad described the basement apartment as "ground level."
   receptive   **deceptive**   **recaptured**

10. Rona thought she could _____ her half-hour speech into ten minutes.
    recapitulate   **reciprocate**   **capacity**

B. Use these words in sentences.

1. perceptive _____

2. reciprocity _____

3. capitulate _____

4. captivate _____

5. percipient _____

Vocabulary Practice 13: Word Roots

Word roots: -trud-, -trus-

A **word root** is a word part, or group of letters, that forms the basic part of a word and gives the word its primary meaning. Knowing the meaning of the root can help you determine the meaning of the whole word.

Example: The roots -trud- and -trus- mean "thrust or push." Adding the prefix pro-, meaning "forward," and the suffix -ion, meaning "act or condition of," to -trus- makes protrusion, which means "something that juts or bulges out."

A. Use the prefix and suffix meanings and the root meaning to write the definitions of these words. Then, check your definitions in a dictionary.

Prefixes and Their Meanings	Suffixes and Their Meanings
pro- "forward"	-er "one who is or does"
ob- "over, against, toward"	-ion "act or condition of"
in- "into"	-ness "act or quality"
abs "from, away"	-ive "of, relating to"
	-ile "suitable for"

1. obtrusive _____

2. intrusion _____

3. protrusion _____

4. intrusive _____

5. obtruded _____

6. intrude _____

7. abstruse _____

8. protruded _____

9. abstruseness _____

10. protrusile _____

B. Use the words in Exercise A to complete the sentences.

1. The air conditioner _____ precariously from the window ledge.

2. Betsy resisted the urge to read her sister's diary; it would be too _____.

3. The historian's _____ speech was replete with specialized vocabulary.

4. Tony interrupted his parents' conversation, saying, "I'm sorry for the _____."

5. Dee's _____ aunt arrived uninvited and stayed for days before the wedding.

6. An elephant's trunk is a _____ because it can be used to grab objects.

7. The spectators were annoyed by the _____ of the players' argument.

8. Jon's brother always tried to _____ in conversations with his friends.

9. A _____ in the back of an open truck must be flagged to alert other drivers.

10. Driving with the top down, the radio sound _____ upon the quiet country air.

C. On another piece of paper, write the meanings of these words and use them in sentences:
intruder, intrusiveness, protrusive, obtruding, abstrusely.

Vocabulary Practice 14: Prefixes, Suffixes, and Word Roots

A **prefix** is a word part added to the beginning of a word. A **suffix** is a word part added to the end of a word. A **word root** is a word part, or group of letters, that forms the basic part of a word. If you know the meanings of prefixes, suffixes, and word roots, you can figure out the meanings of whole words.

A. Using this chart of prefixes, roots, and suffixes, write the definitions for the words below the chart. Check your definitions in a dictionary.

Prefixes	Roots	Suffixes
ex-, e-, ef- "from, out" *di-, dis-* "opposite, apart, away" *ob-* "in the way, against" *ab-* "away from" *co-, con-, com-, col-, cor-* "with, together" _____ _____ _____ _____ _____	*-fac-, -fact-, -fect-, -fic-* "do or make" *-flect-, -flex-, -ang-* "bend" *-frag-, -fract-* "break" *-ject-* "throw" *-cap-, -capt-, -cept-, -cip-* "take, seize, hold" *-trud-, -trus-* "thrust, push" _____ _____ _____	*-ity, -ty, -y* "state or quality of" *-ance, -ence, -ency, -ant, -ent* "act or state of" *-ry, -ery* "state or quality of" *-ary* "related to" *-ic, -etic, -ical, -al* "of, like, related to" *-ion* "act or condition of" *-ure* "action or process" _____ _____ _____

1. extrusion _____

2. complacency _____

3. abstinence _____

4. objectivity _____

5. dejection _____

6. exceptional _____

7. effluence _____

8. fragility _____

9. deception _____

10. conjecture _____

B. Add other prefixes, word roots, and suffixes to the chart. On a separate page, create words by combining the word parts in your chart. Then, write the definitions of the words.

Vocabulary Practice 15: Synonyms

A **synonym** is a word with the same or nearly the same meaning as another word.

Example: The word *strife* is a synonym for the word *conflict*.

A. Match each word in **boldface** with a synonym by writing the letter of the synonym after the word. Then, write another synonym for each word. Check your words in a dictionary or thesaurus.

Words	Synonyms	Synonyms
1. **gambol** _____	a. confuse	_____
2. **abeyance** _____	b. eagerness	_____
3. **fetid** _____	c. involve	_____
4. **largess** _____	d. stubborn	_____
5. **wan** _____	e. reserve	_____
6. **corpulence** _____	f. discontinuance	_____
7. **verdant** _____	g. putrid	_____
8. **mettle** _____	h. clarity	_____
9. **malapropism** _____	i. colorless	_____
10. **alacrity** _____	j. obesity	_____
11. **implicate** _____	k. frolic	_____
12. **diffidence**_____	l. misusage	_____
13. **obfuscate** _____	m. ardor	_____
14. **obstinate** _____	n. green	_____
15. **lucidity** _____	o. generosity	_____

B. Write ten of the boldface words from Exercise A in the sentences.

1. When night fell, the forest elves and fairies would _____ in the moonlight.

2. The parade's _____ was ordered by the Town Council.

3. The _____ swampland was caused by chemical dumping.

4. The Farleys were known among charity circles for their _____.

5. Toby's face was _____ and expressionless when he heard about the accident.

6. The audience was amazed at the _____ of the Sumo wrestlers.

7. After the rain, the forest looked lush and _____.

8. The trainer needed patience, control, and _____ to handle the unruly dog.

9. Lana couldn't hold a conversation without a _____ or two.

10. Sal began his first varsity game at shortstop with _____ and optimism.

C. On separate paper, write a sentence for each of the five words *not* used in Exercise B.

Vocabulary Practice 16: Synonyms

A **synonym** is a word with the same or nearly the same meaning as another word.

Example: The word *aberration* is a synonym for *deviation*.

A. Underline the word in each sentence that is a synonym for the boldface word. Then write a sentence using the boldface word.

1. The principal admonished several students for their offensive behavior.

   reprimanded _____

2. Charlie was disaffected by his family's announcement regarding their relocation.

   malcontent _____

3. Despite her doctor's warnings, Trish was overindulgent on her vacation.

   unconstrained _____

4. Alan's diffidence resulted from being an only child, raised by protective parents.

   insecurity _____

5. The typewriter was a precursor to the teletypewriter, which sent messages by telephone
   and telegraph.

   forerunner _____

6. Mrs. Hanley was effusive about her precocious child, who was also disrespectful.

   exceptional _____

7. The coach tried to ameliorate the relationship between students and faculty.

   rectify _____

8. Dylan liked to pepper his conversation with platitudes to irritate his friends.

   clichés _____

9. Joanne has a proclivity to being a spendthrift, which she may regret.

   tendency _____

10. The clerk's arrogance compared favorably to the customer's audacity.

    brazenness _____

B. Write a brief definition for each word.

1. **reprimanded** _____
2. **rectify** _____
3. **brazenness** _____
4. **malcontent** _____
5. **unconstrained** _____
6. **insecurity** _____
7. **forerunner** _____
8. **exceptional** _____
9. **clichés** _____
10. **tendency** _____

Vocabulary Practice 17: Synonyms

A **synonym** is a word with the same or nearly the same meaning as another word.

Example: The word *continuous* is a synonym for *uninterrupted*.

A. Underline the word in each sentence that is a synonym for the boldface word. Then, write another synonym for the boldface word.

1. Kelly was vigilant about the safety of her younger sister especially when visiting the city.

   guarded _____

2. Normally decisive and positive, Don was ambivalent about the job offer.

   determined _____

3. The coach was vehement about the rules for practice and diet during the football season.

   earnest _____

4. Mabel's absence from the meeting was an aberration that everyone noticed since she was always present. **exception** _____

5. No one could figure out the professor's academic lecture; it certainly was obtuse.

   dull _____

6. Jaws of life were used to extricate the entangled accident victims.

   withdraw _____

7. Nelson was an expatriate and wanted to return to his native country.

   exile _____

8. It was three decades since the classmates had seen each other, so memories of their friendship eluded them. **escaped** _____

9. Students became complacent after the departure of their enthusiastic teacher.

   indifferent _____

10. Dr. Zane liked to dazzle his students with rhetorical questions and their expressions amused him. **elaborate** _____

11. Classmates did not anticipate Todd's droll reading of his prosaic writings.

    mundane _____

12. The puppy collected a conglomeration of insignificant items under the sofa.

    assortment _____

13. There was no justification for the tardiness of the guests to the reception.

    explanation _____

14. Joshua was an erudite, ambitious young man, destined to reach his highest goals.

    educated _____

15. The contract delineated specific requirements for deadlines and payments.

    outlined _____

B. On another piece of paper, write a sentence using each boldface word in Exercise A.

Vocabulary Practice 18: Antonyms

An **antonym** is a word that is opposite in meaning to another word.

Example: The word *boisterous* is an antonym for the word *quiet*.

A. Underline the word in each sentence that is an antonym for the boldface word. Then, write a sentence using the underlined word.

1. The extemporaneous speech by the young orator was more impressive than the carefully **prepared** remarks by his mentor.

_____

2. Jen's blithe spirit is a sharp contrast to her twin brother's **gloomy** demeanor.

_____

3. To make soil richer, more **productive,** farmers allow land to lie fallow for years.

_____

4. My parents are dubious, but Jill's are **positive** about our driving across country.

_____

5. The accused was absolved of wrongdoing and someone else was **implicated.**

_____

6. Northern gardeners prefer hardy plants to **fragile** ones that cannot survive frosts.

_____

7. Karen's broken leg was an inauspicious beginning to an otherwise **favorable** year.

_____

8. One candidate's injurious tactics and the other's **inoffensive** ones were publicized.

_____

9. Our vacation plans are still nebulous because unexpected guests prevent our making them **specific.** _____

10. People wearing seatbelts are unscathed; those who are **unprotected** are injured.

_____

B. Write an antonym for each boldface word. Then, write a sentence using each phrase.

1. **tenuous** evidence _____

2. **dispassionate** spectators _____

3. **enigmatic** smile _____

4. **impetuous** child _____

5. coach's **laxity** _____

Vocabulary Practice 19: Antonyms

An **antonym** is a word that is opposite in meaning to another word.

Example: The word *paragon* is an antonym for the word *pariah*.

A. Match each boldface word with an antonym. Write the letter of the antonym before the word. Then, write another antonym for each boldface word.

	Word	Antonym	Antonym
____	1. **plaintive**	a. compliant	_____
____	2. **effrontery**	b. structured	_____
____	3. **discursive**	c. terse	_____
____	4. **resilient**	d. lengthiness	_____
____	5. **lassitude**	e. focused	_____
____	6. **zenith**	f. ineffective	_____
____	7. **veracity**	g. one-sided	_____
____	8. **multifarious**	h. bottom	_____
____	9. **amorphous**	i. courtesy	_____
____	10. **loquacious**	j. energy	_____
____	11. **malign**	k. brittle	_____
____	12. **recalcitrant**	l. insincerity	_____
____	13. **aggrandize**	m. jubilant	_____
____	14. **efficacious**	n. condense	_____
____	15. **brevity**	o. praise	_____

B. Write ten of the boldface words from Exercise A in the sentences.

1. The _____ lecture was rambling and hard to follow.

2. Nolan had never encountered such _____ from a new and inexperienced employee.

3. With three straight championships, the Blazers were at their _____.

4. Julio's writing was characterized by _____, forthrightness, and zeal.

5. Jill liked dancewear made from fabric that was lightweight and _____.

6. The design for the new town park seemed _____ and ill-planned.

7. Carla developed an _____ ad campaign to reach a variety of customers.

8. The wolves' _____ howls sounded like mourners at a funeral.

9. Basketball practice left Mary in a state of weakness and _____.

10. The scientist was known for the clarity and _____ of his reports.

C. On other paper, write a sentence using each boldface word *not* used in Exercise B.

Vocabulary Practice 20: Antonyms

An **antonym** is a word that is opposite in meaning to another word.

Example: The word *taciturn* is an antonym for the word *communicative*.

A. Write two antonyms for each boldface word. Then, write a sentence using the boldface word.

egoistic	befriended	donate	stingy	unspoiled
commend	spotless	succinct	plain	mischievous
terse	deflect	pale	separate	hospitable
praise	pliable	nasty	obedient	disentangle

1. **desolate** _____ _____

_____

2. **garner** _____ _____

_____

3. **voluble** _____ _____

_____

4. **marred** _____ _____

_____

5. **altruistic** _____ _____

_____

6. **enmesh** _____ _____

_____

7. **florid** _____ _____

_____

8. **lampoon** _____ _____

_____

9. **recalcitrant** _____ _____

_____

10. **cherubic** _____ _____

_____

B. Substitute an antonym for the boldface word in each phrase. Then, use the new phrase in a sentence. Use a dictionary or thesaurus, if necessary

1. **adroit** craftsman _____

2. **deprecatory** stares _____

3. **elegiac** speech _____

4. **lithe** dancer _____

5. **poignant** moment _____

Vocabulary Practice 21: Synonym and Antonym Review

A **synonym** is a word with the same or nearly the same meaning as another word. An **antonym** is a word that is opposite in meaning to another word.

Example: A synonym for *appease* is *placate*. An antonym for *appease* is *provoke*.

A. Write a synonym and an antonym for the boldfaced word in each sentence.

1. Katya was **thoughtless** when she said her little sister's dress was babyish.

   synonym: _____   antonym: _____

2. Saul could hear the sound of **jocularity** coming from the party in the gym.

   synonym: _____   antonym: _____

3. The mid-July Sunday dawned hazy, hot, and **humid.**

   synonym: _____   antonym: _____

4. Neighbors **condemned** the school committee for failing to repair North High.

   synonym: _____   antonym: _____

5. The movie was more than three hours long, but yet, it was very **engrossing.**

   synonym: _____   antonym: _____

6. Cindy thought that PhotoCorp and Pix Co. should **merge** into one company.

   synonym: _____   antonym: _____

7. Sandy was in the **forefront** of his school's volunteer team for the food drive.

   synonym: _____   antonym: _____

8. Summit Avenue runs **perpendicular** to Beacon Street.

   synonym: _____   antonym: _____

9. With extreme **caution,** Jim moved slowly as he learned to rollerblade.

   synonym: _____   antonym: _____

10. Donna was extremely **frugal** when it came to spending money on clothes.

    synonym: _____   antonym: _____

B. Write two synonyms and two antonyms for the boldface words. Use a thesaurus to check your answers.

1. **compliant**   synonyms: _____   antonyms: _____
2. **alacrity**   synonyms: _____   antonyms: _____
3. **veracity**   synonyms: _____   antonyms: _____
4. **assurance**   synonyms: _____   antonyms: _____
5. **aggrandize** synonyms: _____   antonyms: _____
6. **nebulous**   synonyms: _____   antonyms: _____
7. **callow**   synonyms: _____   antonyms: _____
8. **denounce**   synonyms: _____   antonyms: _____
9. **officious**   synonyms: _____   antonyms: _____
10. **redundant** synonyms: _____   antonyms: _____

Vocabulary Practice 22: Analogies

An **analogy** shows a relationship, or makes a comparison, between pairs of words. In an analogy, the relationship between the first pair of words is compared to the relationship in the second pair of words.

Example: One type of relationship is a *function* relationship. In EAR:HEAR::EYE:SEE, "hear" and "see" are functions of "ear" and "eye."

Example: Another type of analogy shows a *cause-effect* relationship. In BURN:PAIN::SLEEP:REST, "burn" causes "pain," and "sleep" causes "rest."

A. Determine the relationship between the first pair of words. Then write the word that completes the second pair of words in the analogy.

1. NEWS:DESCRIPTION::COMMERCIAL:_____

   a. influence   b. information   c. capitalism

2. PAUCITY:HUNGER::DISCIPLINE:_____

   a. sharpen   b. order   c. command

3. ANESTHETIC:NUMB::LEAVEN:_____

   a. complete   b. equalize   c. raise

4. LIGAMENT:CONNECT::ADDENDUM:_____

   a. supplement   b. discharge   c. change

5. COMPROMISE:SOLUTION::ANCHOR:_____

   a. stability   b. dissipation   c. retention

6. FLOOD:DESTRUCTION::CURMUDGEON:_____

   a. confusion   b. lenience   c. discord

7. EATING:SATIATION::FORGERY:_____

   a. sympathy   b. beguilement   c. spontaneity

8. LANGUAGE:COMMUNICATION::PRACTICE:_____

   a. mistakes   b. performance   c. perfection

9. DISUSE:ATROPHY::DROUGHT:_____

   a. polyphony   b. thirst   c. growth

10. DINGHY:TRANSPORT::TIRADE:_____

   a. denounce   b. venerate   c. exclaim

B. Write a word to complete these analogies.

1. TRAVESTY:RIDICULE::RADIATOR:_____

2. PERFIDY:MISTRUST::VIRUS:_____

3. UNCERTAINTY:HESITATION::DISINTEREST:_____

4. EXPLANATION:AMELIORATE::INSULATION:_____

5. FOOD:NOURISHMENT::HELMET:_____

C. On another piece of paper, rewrite the first pair of words in each analogy in Exercise B.

Vocabulary Practice 23: Analogies

An **analogy** shows a relationship, or makes a comparison, between pairs of words. In an analogy, the relationship between the first pair of words is compared to the relationship in the second pair of words. Writing a summary sentence that explains the relationship between the first pair of words can help to clarify the word relationship.

Example: QUILT:BED::ASPHALT:_____. Summary sentence: "You use a quilt to cover a bed." What do you use *asphalt* for? The word *driveway* would complete this analogy.

A. Think about the relationship between each pair of words. On the line below each analogy, write a sentence that explains the relationship between the words in the first pair. Then, write a word to complete the second pair of words in the analogy.

1. COMPETITION:WINNER::BUSINESS:_____

   _____

2. TRUDGE:WALK::BACKSTROKE:_____

   _____

3. ZIPPER:FASTENER::HELIUM:_____

   _____

4. RING:MARRIAGE::CROWN:_____

   _____

5. PROFESSOR:UNIVERSITY::ARTIST:_____

   _____

6. ELATION:HAPPINESS::GLOOM:_____

   _____

7. HOT AIR:BALLOON::ENGINE:_____

   _____

8. SORROW:TEARS::HAPPINESS:_____

   _____

9. EXPERT:NOVICE::SENIOR:_____

   _____

10. TURN:DOORKNOB::PULL:_____

   _____

B. Determine the relationship in the first pair of words. Write a word that completes the second pair of words in each analogy.

1. RECLINER:CHAIR::MAPLE:_____

2. MALODOROUS:FRAGRANT::COMPRESSED: _____

3. PLAYERS:DUGOUT::FAMILY:_____

4. STAMINA:MARATHONER::PATIENCE:_____

5. STAR:CONSTELLATION::TRIBUTARY:_____

Vocabulary Practice 24: Analogies

An **analogy** shows a relationship, or makes a comparison, between pairs of words. In an analogy, the relationship between the first pair of words is compared to the relationship in the second pair of words. Types of analogies include *function, cause-effect, synonym/antonym,* and *part to whole* relationships.

Examples: TRANSMITTER:COMMUNICATE::MICROSCOPE:MAGNIFY (function)
FUMES: INTOXICATION::OVEREXPOSURE:SUNBURN (cause-effect)
DISSENSION:ACCORD::ELEGIAC:JOYOUS (synonym/antonym)
KEY:KEYBOARD::WING:AIRCRAFT (part to whole)

A. Circle the letter before the pair or words that completes each analogy.

1. DUPLICITY: MISTRUST::_____
   a. scissors:rent
   b. enthrall:mesmerize
   c. employment:remuneration

2. ENGENDER:CAUSE::_____
   a. compass:navigate
   b. hiatus:interruption
   c. nightmare:awakening

3. INDULGENCE:CORPULENCE::_____
   a. hardy:robust
   b. negotiation:concordance
   c. constrict:release

4. MALLET:PULVERIZE::_____
   a. catapult:jettison
   b. socket:chandelier
   c. zenith:mountain

5. DESPOIL:LOOT::_____
   a. cylinder:engine
   b. terse:discursive
   c. lampoon:satirize

6. CUTLERY:MINCE::_____
   a. diminish:reduce
   b. bacteria:infection
   c. jail:sequester

7. STRIDENT:SOOTHING::_____
   a. taciturn:boisterous
   b. electricity:lightning
   c. svelte:slim

8. ELECTROCARDIOGRAM:MEASUREMENT::_____
   a. surly:rude
   b. calculator:compute
   c. sprocket:wheel

9. NUTRITION:HEALTH::_____
   a. narrative:exposition
   b. resonant:ringing
   c. aging:wrinkles

10. VIRULENT:TOXIC::_____
    a. appropriate:timely
    b. wan:colorful
    c. stomach:digest

11. MEDICATION:ILLNESS::_____
    a. bliss:despondency
    b. fission:fusion
    c. accident:injury

12. PHYSICIAN:HEAL::_____
    a. bungle:succeed
    b. capitalist:finance
    c. hospital:patient

13. BANAL:EXTRAORDINARY::_____
    a. hyperbole:understatement
    b. copious:profuse
    c. liquid:hydrate

14. DETECTIVE:INVESTIGATE::_____
    a. coddle:spoil
    b. clue:mystery
    c. handcuffs:shackle

15. CONDENSATION:PRECIPITATION::_____
    a. copyright:protection
    b. arrest:confinement
    c. hurricane:typhoon

B. On a separate page, write one example for each type of analogy.

Vocabulary Practice 25: Connotations and Denotations

A **connotation** is the implied or suggested meaning of a word or phrase. It is different from the **denotation,** or dictionary definition. Words with the same denotation convey different connotations, depending on the use in context.

A. Complete the sentences with two of the given words.

1. Words that connote "equality" are *identical, equivalent,* and *corresponding.*
   a. Michelle asked what the word _____ to the English "internet" was in French.
   b. Greg and Harry's expensive, new basketball sneakers were _____.

2. Words that connote "an end" are *termination, culmination,* and *expiration.*
   a. Tucker wondered about the _____ date of his freelance contract.
   b. The high school dance was the _____ of six months of fund-raising.

3. Words that connote "something new" are *fresh, modern,* and *innovative.*
   a. Weary of the year's boring designs, the company was seeking a _____ look.
   b. Trent's unheard-of campaign idea was a truly _____ idea.

4. Words that connote "degrees of time" are *often, continual,* and *common.*
   a. Connie thought she got stuck with dishwashing chores all too _____.
   b. Ms. Watson told her class that tornadoes were a _____ occurrence in Kansas.
   c. _____

5. Words that connote "types of power" are *potency, force,* and *energy.*
   a. Wilton Veras hit his first homerun over the wall with great _____.
   b. Marianne told her cousin that her brand of vitamins had greater _____.

6. Words that connote "types of travel" are *tour, trek,* and *migration.*
   a. Thousands of geese headed south from Canada on their annual _____.
   b. Brenda and her boyfriend wanted to take a _____ of the state capitol.

7. Words that connote "degrees of rainfall" are *downpour, sprinkle,* and *shower.*
   a. With the prediction of a serious _____, people worried about flooding.
   b. The Cohens' outing was in question because of the possibility of a _____.

8. Words that connote "to judge" are *assess, discriminate,* and *censure.*
   a. Dean postponed interviewing until he'd had time to _____ the candidates.
   b. Holly found it difficult to _____ between the various shades of light blue.

9. Words that connote "hope" are *expectation, promise,* and *faith.*
   a. Nancy had _____ that her friends would come through for her.
   b. Alan's spirits soared with the _____ of a beautiful day.

10. Words that connote "types of news" are *information, intelligence,* and *report.*
    a. The Copellos worried because they'd had no _____ from their son in days.
    b. Brandy turned on the television to get a _____ on the shuttle launch.

B. On another piece of paper, write a sentence using the remaining words in Exercise A.

Vocabulary Practice 26: Connotations and Denotations

A **connotation** is the implied or suggested meaning of a word or phrase. Connotations convey implied meanings and are positive, neutral, or negative, depending on the text.

Example: *Inquire* and *snoop* have the same denotative meaning, "to be curious." *Inquire* has a positive or neutral connotation, meaning "to ask." *Snoop* has a negative connotation, meaning "to pry into the private affairs of others."

A. This list of words are connotations for *sullen*. Choose and write three words that could complete each sentence and convey the appropriate connotation for the text. You may use some words more than once.

bad-tempered, churlish, crabby, cross, cynical, dismal, dour, fretful, frowning, gloomy, glowering, glum, gruff, grumpy, hostile, irritable, mean, moody, obstinate, pouting, somber, silent, sulking, unsociable

1. Kitty was usually a very cheerful person, but on Monday morning when she could not find her contact lenses, she was _____.

2. The clerk was positively _____ towards the customer, creating a scene in the store by raising her voice and waving her arms in the customer's face.

3. After school, Chris received the disappointing news about his loan application and this turned his cheerful smile into a _____ demeanor.

4. Lulu was a handful. Her mother tried everything to coax the five-year-old to eat her dinner. Lulu not only would not eat, but she sat at the table with her arms folded and a _____ expression on her face.

5. After a long, hot day excavating the road, the men were asked to work an extra hour. Some were agreeable, but the majority spoke to their bosses in angry, _____ tones and their body language displayed their unhappy mood.

B. Choose one of the sentences in Exercise A as a topic sentence, and write a paragraph that uses at least three of the boldface words listed in Exercise A. Underline the words you use.

_____

_____

_____

_____

_____

_____

_____

_____

_____

_____

_____

_____

Vocabulary Practice 27: Connotations and Denotations

A **connotation** is the implied or suggested meaning of a word or phrase. Connotations convey implied meanings, positive, negative, or neutral, depending on the text.

Example: *Welcome* and *accost* have the same denotative meaning, "to greet." *Welcome* has a positive or neutral connotation, meaning "greet" (neutral) or "greet favorably" (positive). *Accost* has a negative connotation, meaning "greet in a challenging way."

A. Write the two words that are connotations for each boldface word. Then, identify all the words as positive, neutral, or negative connotations. Last, write a sentence using one word in each set. Check your words in a dictionary or thesaurus.

reluctance	terse	ornate	unruly	spontaneous
mercy	insincerity	sharpen	argumentative	hone
unplanned	compact	innocent	tawdry	hostile
obstinate	deception	aversion	compassion	unsophisticated

Word	Connotation	Word/Connotation	Word/Connotation
1. **whet**	_____	_____	_____
2. **callow**	_____	_____	_____
3. **extemporaneous**	_____	_____	_____
4. **polemical**	_____	_____	_____
5. **intractable**	_____	_____	_____
6. **garish**	_____	_____	_____
7. **duplicity**	_____	_____	_____
8. **laconic**	_____	_____	_____
9. **clemency**	_____	_____	_____
10. **diffidence**	_____	_____	_____

B. On another piece of paper, rewrite each sentence you wrote in Exercise A using a word with a different connotation. Underline the connotation for the boldface word.

Name _____ Date _____

Vocabulary Practice 28: Commonly Misused Words

Having a good vocabulary demands skillful use of the right words in speaking and writing. Many words and phrases sound alike. Other words cause confusion because their meanings are not understood.

Example: *They're, their,* and *there* sound alike, but have different meanings and uses.

A. Write the word or phrase that completes each sentence.

1. The final _____ of the daily newspaper is printed at midnight.
   edition, addition

2. On the _____ from the mountain, the climbers became dizzy and were rescued.
   decent, descent

3. Susie wanted to _____ her dress because it did not fit after losing weight. **alter, altar**

4. How often have you wanted to voice your _____ opinion in a tense situation? **personal, personnel**

5. Along the coast, we saw the sea otters _____ from the water to lie on the rocks. **immerse, emerge**

6. The grocery sign correctly noted that those with _____ ten items could use aisle one. **fewer than, less than**

7. People are often unaware that their _____ remarks are offensive to some people. **callous, callus**

8. Dorothy was _____ because she was unprepared for her final exams.
   anxious, eager

9. Mr. Bolger was the _____ for the plaintiff and won the case.
   council, counsel

10. The senator said the charter was _____ the one written many hundred years ago. **different from, different than**

11. Carol _____ until she had all the signatures on the petition.
    canvases, canvassed

12. Mother will _____ us on time to depart for the weekend celebration.
    anticipate, expect

13. New owners of the store will take over when the current owners _____ control.
    cease, seize

14. With insufficient information, the speaker _____ before his audience. **floundered, foundered**

15. Our money will go _____ if we plan wisely before we begin spending it.
    farther, further

B. On another piece of paper, write a sentence using each word you did *not* use in the sentences in Exercise A.

Vocabulary Practice 29: Commonly Misused Words

Having a good vocabulary demands skillful use of the right words in speaking and writing. Many words and phrases sound alike and cause confusion.

Example: *Capital* and *capitol* sound alike, but have different meanings and uses.

A. Write the word that completes each sentence.

sure	adapt	dessert	desert	base
imply	precede	waver	avenge	already
certainly	all ready	deductive	bass	revenge
adopt	infer	waiver	inductive	proceed

1. Before she ordered _____, Kendra considered the effect of pie on

   her waistline.

2. Brian planned to _____ the celebratory dinner with an introductory speech.

3. HiCo. hadn't installed Tai's phone properly, so it granted him a fee _____.

4. In his opening statement, the prosecutor asserted that the motive was _____.

5. Before her party, Rory adjusted the treble and _____ levels on her speakers.

6. When his wife asked him to prepare the meal, Marc said, "_____, Dear."

7. Tenley inquired if her children would be _____ to go to the picnic by noon.

8. From her boyfriend's morose look, Gia could _____ he'd failed the exam.

9. The terrain was more rugged than she'd expected, but Dena could _____ to it.

10. Dr. Perry used _____ reasoning to draw conclusions from the available facts.

B. Write a definition for each word you used in the sentences in Exercise A. Check your definitions in a dictionary.

1. _____

2. _____

3. _____

4. _____

5. _____

6. _____

7. _____

8. _____

9. _____

10. _____

C. On another piece of paper, write a sentence using each word you did *not* use in Exercise A.

Vocabulary Practice 30: Commonly Misused Words

Having a good vocabulary demands skillful use of the right words in speaking and writing. Many words and phrases sound alike and cause confusion.

Example: *Stationary* and *stationery* sound alike, but have different meanings and uses.

A. Write the word or phrase that completes each sentence. Then, write a sentence using the other word in each pair.

1. The critic implied that the acting in the new play was _____ too unrehearsed.
   all together, altogether

   _____

2. The malodorous condition of Roy's wet poodle was bound to _____ people.
   repulse, repel

   _____

3. Nell was quite _____ at sports, perhaps because her dad coached gymnastics.
   adapt, adept

   _____

4. Ted studied diligently, but the trigonometry answers managed to _____ him.
   allude, elude

   _____

5. The district attorney boasted he had enough evidence to _____ the suspect.
   persecute, prosecute

   _____

6. Try as she might, Mrs. Dahl couldn't _____ her son to apply for a summer job.
   impel, propel

   _____

7. The heckler added a note of _____ to an otherwise cordial town meeting.
   descent, dissent

   _____

8. When Sara revealed the surprising results of her study, her peers were _____.
   incredible, incredulous

   _____

9. Kit's community rent-control petition was met with indifference and _____.
   apathy, empathy

   _____

10. Lexi aided the whelping of her beagle's four pups—all born alive and _____.
    healthful, healthy

    _____

B. On another piece of paper, write a definition for the boldface words in Exercise A.

Vocabulary Practice 31: Specialized Vocabulary

Most of the words we use today have their origins in Old English, Latin, and Greek. Many Latin phrases are used in speaking and writing.

A. Using a dictionary, write the definition of each term. Then, write a sentence using each term.

1. *ad hoc* _____
   _____

2. *pro bono* _____
   _____

3. *ad nauseam* _____
   _____

4. *caveat emptor* _____
   _____

5. *de facto* _____
   _____

6. *ex officio* _____
   _____

7. *habeas corpus* _____
   _____

8. *ipso facto* _____
   _____

9. *non sequitur* _____
   _____

10. *pro forma* _____
    _____

11. *carpe diem* _____
    _____

12. *per diem* _____
    _____

13. *status quo* _____
    _____

14. *sine die* _____
    _____

15. *nolo contendere* _____
    _____

B. Which three phrases are legal terminology?

_____

Vocabulary Practice 32: Specialized Vocabulary

Many of the musical terms we use today have their origins in Latin and have been borrowed from contemporary Italian.

A. Using a dictionary, write the definition of each musical term. Then, write each term in the box under the correct classification.

1. *adagio* _____

2. *allegro* _____

3. *andante* _____

4. *aria* _____

5. *basso* _____

6. *coloratura* _____

7. *concerto* _____

8. *crescendo* _____

9. *dolce* _____

10. *fortissimo* _____

11. *presto* _____

12. *sonata* _____

13. *soprano* _____

14. *staccato* _____

15. *tempo* _____

Type of Composition	Type of Voice	Style or Volume of Music	Relative Speed of Music

B. On another piece of paper, write a sentence for each musical term in Exercise A.

Spelling Practice 1: Adding Prefixes

When a **prefix** is added to a word, the spelling of the word remains the same. In some words, adding a prefix to a word results in a doubled consonant.

Examples: The prefix *in-* added to *sensitive* makes *insensitive*. The prefix *mis-* added to *spell* makes *misspell*. Adding *il-* to *legal* makes *illegal*.

A. Combine the prefixes and words and write the new words. Then, write another word with the same prefix.

1. *pro-* and *democracy* makes _____ _____
2. *a-* and *typical* makes _____ _____
3. *dis-* and *passionate* makes _____ _____
4. *pre-* and *meditated* makes _____ _____
5. *im-* and *pious* makes _____ _____
6. *in-* and *conceivable* makes _____ _____
7. *un-* and *documented* makes _____ _____
8. *dis-* and *satisfactory* makes _____ _____
9. *re-* and *route* makes _____ _____
10. *anti-* and *discrimination* makes _____ _____
11. *pro-* and *active* makes _____ _____
12. *a-* makes *moral* makes _____ _____
13. *dis-* and *credited* makes _____ _____
14. *im-* and *plausible* makes _____ _____
15. *non-* and *negotiable* makes _____ _____

B. Write these misspelled words correctly. Check your answers in a dictionary. Then, write a brief definition for each word.

1. imutable _____
2. ilimitable _____
3. inumerable _____
4. disatisfactory _____
5. imodest _____
6. disimilar _____
7. imortalize _____
8. ireverent _____
9. unoticeable _____
10. disoluble _____
11. efervescent _____
12. unerved _____
13. iresponsible _____
14. disipated _____
15. iliterate _____

Spelling Practice 2: Adding Suffixes

When adding suffixes to words ending in final *e*, follow the rules for dropping or keeping *e*.

Spelling Rules

1. When adding a suffix that begins with a vowel to a word that ends in *e*, drop the final *e*.

   Example: The suffix *-ing* added to *efface* makes *effacing*.

2. When adding a suffix that begins with a consonant to a word that ends in *e*, keep the final *e*.

   Example: The suffix *-ment* added to *announce* makes *announcement*.

A. Combine the words and suffixes and write the new words.

1. *disparage* and *-ing* _____
2. *furtive* and *-ness* _____
3. *emulate* and *-ive* _____
4. *recognize* and *-able* _____
5. *animate* and *-ion* _____
6. *immediate* and *-ly* _____
7. *fickle* and *-ness* _____
8. *coddle* and *-ing* _____
9. *dispassionate* and *-ly* _____
10. *extradite* and *-ion* _____
11. *discursive* and *-ness* _____
12. *bungle* and *-er* _____
13. *exonerate* and *-ive* _____
14. *desecrate* and *-ion* _____
15. *ostracize* and *-ing* _____

B. Underline the misspelled word in each sentence. Write the word correctly at the end of the sentence. Check your spelling in a dictionary.

1. Julia was in a state of bereavment after the death of her best friend. _____
2. When Jen discovered she had spread harmful rumors, she acted contritly. _____
3. Robin began hedgeing when her parents asked why she had not called home. _____
4. Brad's refuseal to work overtime was not acceptable to his supervisor. _____
5. The aerobics class was rejuvenateing for everyone who had sat through hours of classes.

   _____

6. The professor was venerateed by his students because he was a mentor to them.

   _____

7. The reporter's delineateion of the story facts was corroborated by the eyewitnesses.

   _____

8. As he sat holding his brother's broken bat, Earle hoped for forgivness. _____
9. Leah's father worried about his daughter's espouseal of radical ideas. _____
10. Della's personality tended toward rudness when she was feeling hurried. _____

C. Write two words that are examples of the spelling rules for adding suffixes to words ending in final *e*.

_____

_____

_____

Spelling Practice 2: Adding Suffixes

When adding suffixes to words with final *y*, follow spelling rules for keeping *y* or changing *y* to *i* before adding the suffix.

Spelling Rules

1. Change *y* to *i* in words ending with a consonant plus *y* before adding suffixes *-ness*, *-er*, *-ed*, *-ly*, and *-ous*.

Example: Adding *-ness* to *hazy* makes *haziness*.

2. Change *y* to *i* before adding suffixes *-ance*, *-ant*, and *-able*.

Example: Adding *-ance* to *apply* makes *appliance*.

3. Keep the final *y* in words ending with a vowel plus *y* before suffixes *-er*, *-ous*, *-ance*, *-ing*, *-ful*, and *-ness*.

Example: Adding *-er* to *buy* makes *buyer*.

4. Keep the final *y* when adding the suffixes *-ing* or *-ish* to avoid having two *i*'s.

Example: Adding *-ing* to *try* makes *trying*.

D. If the word is spelled correctly, put a check (√) beside the word. Write the misspelled words correctly. Check your answers in a dictionary.

1. categorycally _____
2. pitying _____
3. surlyest _____
4. merryment _____
5. prettyly _____
6. chillyness _____
7. sorryest _____
8. tidyer _____

9. necessaryly _____
10. worrysome _____
11. angrily _____
12. haughtyer _____
13. pithyness _____
14. gayly _____
15. bountyful _____

E. Combine the words and suffixes and write the new words. Then, write another word with the same suffix.

1. *mighty* and *-er* _____
2. *burly* and *-est* _____
3. *extraordinary* and *-ly* _____
4. *shabby* and *-ness* _____
5. *duty* and *-ful* _____
6. *tardy* and *-ly* _____
7. *mystify* and *-ing* _____
8. *embody* and *-ment* _____
9. *uncanny* and *-ly* _____
10. *justify* and *-able* _____
11. *relay* and *-ed* _____
12. *accompany* and *-ment* _____
13. *spongy* and *-ness* _____
14. *simply* and *-fy* _____
15. *sloppy* and *-er* _____

Spelling Practice 3: Words Ending in *ee*
or in a Vowel and Final *e*

When a suffix beginning with *e* is added to a word ending in *ee*, one *e* is dropped. No spelling changes occur when other suffixes are added.

Example: The suffix -*ed* added to *agree* makes *agreed*. The suffix -*ment* added to *agree* makes *agreement*.

A. Combine the words and the suffixes and write the new words.

1. *foresee* and -*ing* _____
2. *wee* and -*est* _____
3. *decree* and -*ed* _____
4. *filigree* and -*es* _____
5. *lee* and -*ward* _____
6. *puree* and -*ed* _____
7. *emcee* and -*ing* _____
8. *pedigree* and -*ed* _____

9. *oversee* and -*ing* _____
10. *free* and -*er* _____
11. *flee* and -*ing* _____
12. *apogee* and -*es* _____
13. *guarantee* and -*ing* _____
14. *absentee* and -*es* _____
15. *disagree* and -*able* _____

B. Underline the misspelled word in each sentence. Write the word correctly at the end of the sentence.

1. The disagreing friends were aided by a supporting friend who interceded.

_____

2. decided to sift the dry ingredients while her mother was pureing the fruit.

_____

3. used washing machine was guaranted to work by the previous owner.

_____

4. refered the basketball games for the high school team for two years.

_____

5. Mrs. Chapman was ecstatic about the artist who had filigreeed the archway.

_____

6. The school committee said that no funds are available in the foreseable future.

_____

7. May and Li shared divergent views and yet were usually in agrement.

_____

8. The children were gleful when they heard the no school announcement.

_____

9. The nomines for the Citizens' Award were Ben and his sister for saving a life.

_____

10. The political club felt fortunate to have two notables for debate emces.

_____

C. Using the dictionary, list as many words as you can find ending in *ee*. Then add suffixes to the words.

Spelling Practice 3: Words Ending in *ee* or in a Vowel and Final *e*

When a suffix beginning with *e* is added to a word ending in *Ve* (vowel + *e*), the final *e* is dropped. When adding other suffixes, different spelling rules apply.

Spelling Rules

1. Keep the final *e* in words ending in *ie* before adding suffixes, except when adding *-ing* and suffixes beginning with *e*. When adding *-ing*, change *ie* to *y*.

   Examples: Adding *-ing* to *tie* makes *tying*. Adding *-less* to *tie* makes *tieless*.

2. Keep the final *e* in words ending in *oe* and *ye* before adding suffixes, except those beginning with *e*.

   Examples: Adding *-ing* to *hoe* makes *hoeing*. Adding *-ed* to *hoe* makes *hoed*.

3. Drop the final *e* in words ending in *ue* before adding suffixes that begin with vowels. Keep the final *e* before adding suffixes that begin with consonants.

   Examples: Adding *-ish* to *blue* makes *bluish*. Adding *-ness* to *blue* makes *blueness*.

D. Add the suffixes to the words and write the new words. Check your spelling in a dictionary.

1. *accrue* and *-ing* _____
2. *woe* and *-ful* _____
3. *vie* and *-ed* _____
4. *issue* and *-able* _____
5. *dye* and *-ed* _____
6. *canoe* and *-ist* _____
7. *pique* and *-ed* _____
8. *argue* and *-able* _____
9. *toe* and *-ing* _____
10. *belie* and *-ed* _____

11. *opaque* and *-ness* _____
12. *tie* and *-ing* _____
13. *ensue* and *-ed* _____
14. *eye* and *-ing* _____
15. *blue* and *-est* _____
16. *true* and *-er* _____
17. *untie* and *-ed* _____
18. *shoe* and *-less* _____
19. *value* and *-able* _____
20. *oblique* and *-ly* _____

E. Categorize the word you wrote in Exercise C according to the spelling rule that applies for adding suffixes to words ending in a vowel and final *e*.

Keep final *e*	Drop final *e*	Change *ie* to *y*
_____	_____	_____
_____	_____	_____
_____	_____	_____
_____	_____	_____
_____	_____	_____
_____	_____	_____
_____	_____	_____
_____	_____	_____
_____	_____	_____
_____	_____	_____

Name _____ Date _____

Spelling Practice 4: Vowels Before Final *r*

Words with a vowel followed by final *r* usually follow rules for spelling.

Spelling Rule: In an unstressed syllable, the vowel sound before the final r is /ə/ and may be spelled by *a, e, i, o,* and *u.*

1. Words ending in ul_r take the vowel *a* as in *regular;* the exception is *ruler.*

2. Words ending in *ate* (regulate) and *ct* (connect) take the vowel *o* when adding *r* as in *regulator* and *connector;* some exceptions are *locater, distracter.*

3. Words meaning "one who does something" take *er* as in *teacher,* or *or* as in *juror.*

A. Add the missing vowel to each word. Check your spelling in a dictionary.

1. engend_r	11. vineg_r	21. occ_r	31. few_r
2. squal_r	12. smuggl_r	22. consum_r	32. protract_r
3. modul_r	13. initiat_r	23. ast_r	33. benefact_r
4. cell_r	14. toddl_r	24. design_r	34. altimet_r
5. centimet_r	15. cloist_r	25. precurs_r	35. serv_r
6. prosecut_r	16. direct_r	26. procrastinat_r	36. conif_r
7. famili_r	17. cellul_r	27. request_r	37. conc_r
8. impost_r	18. edit_r	28. ranc_r	38. inspect_r
9. react_r	19. cartograph_r	29. vap_r	39. val_r
10. indicat_r	20. vehicul_r	30. surrend_r	40. amate_r

B. Organize the words according to the spelling rules in Exercise A.

u/_r	ate, ct	er, or
_____	_____	_____
_____	_____	_____
_____	_____	_____
_____	_____	_____
_____	_____	_____
_____	_____	_____
_____	_____	_____
_____	_____	_____
_____	_____	_____
_____	_____	_____
_____	_____	_____
_____	_____	_____

Spelling Practice 5: Words Ending in *-ise, -ize, -ity, -ety*

Word endings that sound alike are commonly misspelled. The endings *-ise* and *-ize, -ety* and *-ity* are often confused.

Spelling Rules

1. In American English, the predominant ending is *-ize*, except for compound words.

Example: *winterize*

Exceptions: *likewise, otherwise*

2. The ending *-ety* appears when *-ty* is added to certain adjectives ending in *e*.

Examples: *entire, entirety; naïve, naïvety; nice, nicety*

3. The ending *-ety* appears in words ending in *i* to avoid two *i*'s. The ending *ity* is more common.

Examples: *variety, gaiety*

A. Write the misspelled words correctly. Put a check (√) next to the words that are spelled correctly. Check your spelling in a dictionary.

1. politicise _____	11. capsise _____
2. enterprize _____	12. lengthwize _____
3. aggrandize _____	13. advertize _____
4. ostracise _____	14. advize _____
5. merchandise _____	15. popularize _____
6. supervize _____	16. victimise _____
7. pulverise _____	17. guise _____
8. chastize _____	18. criticise _____
9. eulogize _____	19. televize _____
10. compromise _____	20. otherwise _____

B. Write these misspelled words correctly. Check your spelling in a dictionary.

1. disparety _____	11. niceity _____
2. acuety _____	12. sureity _____
3. anxiity _____	13. proclivety _____
4. pugnacety _____	14. impiity _____
5. sobriity _____	15. gaiity _____
6. entireity _____	16. subtleity _____
7. alacrety _____	17. felicety _____
8. hilarety _____	18. impropriity _____
9. notoriity _____	19. variity _____
10. brevety _____	20. receptivety _____

C. On a separate sheet of paper, organize the words in Exercises A and B according to their endings. Then, write the spelling rule that applies to each group of words.

Spelling Practice 6: Words Ending in -c, -k, -ch, -ck, -que

The final sound /k/ is spelled -c, -k, -ch, -ck, and -que.

Spelling Rules

1. The endings -ch and -que with the /k/ sound are used infrequently.

Examples: *stomach, antique, pique*

2. Final -c occurs in the ending -ic and in some words borrowed from other languages.

Examples: *attic, bivouac*

3. The endings -k and -ck appear in words such as *break* and *check*.

4. When adding suffixes beginning with *e, i,* or *y* to words in which the final -c has the /k/ sound, add the letter *k* before the suffix.

Examples: Adding -ed to *mimic* makes *mimicked.* Adding -y to *colic* makes *colicky.* Adding -ing to *picnic* makes *picnicking.*

A. Write the ending for each word. Check your spelling in a dictionary.

bis _____   ironi _____   didacti _____   mimi _____

graph _____   tor _____   politi _____   chron _____

histrion _____   physi _____   trag _____   physi _____

euphoni _____   monar _____   havo _____   intrins _____

mysti _____   maveri _____   organ _____   pani _____

B. Add the endings to these words and write the new words. Then, use a dictionary to find five more words with the final sound /k/.

picnic and *-ing*   *panic* and *-y*   *politic* and *-ing*   *traffic* and *-ed*

mimic and *-ed*   *physic* and *-al*   *antique* and *-es*   *artistic* and *-ally*

logic and *-al*   *frolic* and *-ing*

_____   _____   _____

_____   _____   _____

_____   _____   _____

_____   _____   _____

_____   _____   _____

_____   _____   _____

_____   _____   _____

_____   _____   _____

_____   _____   _____

Spelling Practice 7: Commonly Misspelled Words

Some words follow rules for spelling, while the spelling of other words must be remembered.

Example: Words with *ei* or *ie* follow the rule: *i* before *e* except after *c* or when sounded like *a* as in neighbor and weigh.

A. Write these misspelled words correctly. Check your spelling in a dictionary.

1. mischeivous _____
2. liesure _____
3. cheiftan _____
4. peirce _____
5. percieve _____
6. inconcievable _____
7. foriegn _____
8. hygeine _____

9. riegn _____
10. obiesance _____
11. wierd _____
12. shiek _____
13. plebiean _____
14. niether _____
15. speceis _____

Words ending in *-ish* or *-ist* are often misspelled. The ending *-ish* means "relating to" or describes "an action or process." The ending *-ist* means "one who practices."

Examples: *stylish, nourish, zoologist*

B. Write the ending *-ist* or *-ish* that is added to each word to spell the word that matches the definition. Then, write the new word. Some words change spelling before adding the ending.

Word and Suffix	New Word	Definition
1. *sheep* and _____	_____	timid; bashful
2. *moral* and _____	_____	one who leads a moral life
3. *child* and _____	_____	one who acts like a child
4. *pacify* and _____	_____	one who opposes war
5. *peeve* and _____	_____	marked by bad temper
6. *classic* and _____	_____	a classical scholar
7. *purple* and _____	_____	characteristic of the color purple
8. *churl* and _____	_____	surly; boorish
9. *botany* and _____	_____	a scientist who studies plants
10. *minimal* and _____	_____	one who likes to keep things to a minimum

C. Write ten words that end in *-ish* or *-ist*. Include words for each meaning of *-ish*.

_____

_____

_____

_____

_____

Spelling Practice 8: Commonly Misspelled Words

Some words follow rules for spelling, while other words must be remembered.

A. Add the endings *-ancy, -ency, -cy,* or *-sy* to these words. Then, check your spelling in a dictionary.

-ancy or -ency		*-cy or -sy*	
1. pot _____		embas _____	
2. occup _____		discourte _____	
3. resid _____		pharma _____	
4. complac _____		bankrupt _____	
5. tend _____		biop _____	
6. absorb _____		ecsta _____	
7. clem _____		courte _____	
8. expedi _____		autocra _____	
9. consist _____		prophe _____	
10. resili _____		controver _____	
11. redund _____		accura _____	
12. insolv _____		hypocri _____	
13. depend _____		normal _____	
14. discrep _____		pira _____	
15. dorm _____		idiosyncra _____	
16. effici _____		aristocra _____	
17. frequ _____		jealou _____	
18. hesit _____		falla _____	
19. tru _____		immedia _____	
20. vagr _____		luna _____	

B. Add as many words as you can with each ending. Check your spelling in a dictionary.

-ancy	*-ency*	*-cy*	*-sy*
_____	_____	_____	_____
_____	_____	_____	_____
_____	_____	_____	_____
_____	_____	_____	_____
_____	_____	_____	_____
_____	_____	_____	_____
_____	_____	_____	_____
_____	_____	_____	_____

Spelling Practice 9: Commonly Misspelled Words

Words with endings that sound alike are often misspelled.

A. Underline the misspelled word(s) in each sentence. Write the words correctly at the end of the sentences.

1. Zoe was fasinated by the soler calender that was carved in Summit Park. _____

2. Pete laughed at goulish tales, yet he wouldn't walk through the cemetary. _____

3. Uri's favorite historical subject was Imperial Japan and its regal empirers. _____

4. As June's older sister, it was essental for Jan to be a good role moddal. _____

5. Rhea was mortified because the wine she poured had turned to vineger. _____

6. A high incidance of deafness is a hereditery condition in Dalmatians. _____

7. Dylan's father often let him visit him at the moleculer biology laboratary. _____

8. Cal knew his secretery could perform more than administrative tasks. _____

9. When Beth met Fran's boyfriend, she was convinsed that he looked familier. _____

10. More than fifty sponsers signed up for the charety walk-a-thon.

    _____

11. Mr. Formica travelled so much he couldn't be particuler about his diet. _____

12. All the teachers hopped the layoffs would be a temporery situation. _____

13. Tati refused to feed her puppy table scraps so that he would not be a begger at the table.

    _____

14. Every freshman was in a similur situation at the begining of the term. _____

15. Liz wrote about baseball as a metafor for life in her term paper. _____

B. Write each word correctly. Then place the words under the boldface headings below.

1. horizontial _____   9. theoreticial _____

2. susceptable _____   10. indispensible _____

3. syllible _____   11. municipial _____

4. benefical _____   12. influental _____

5. universial _____   13. inevitible _____

6. permissable _____   14. preferible _____

7. eligable _____   15. irresistable _____

8. pedastial _____

-al	**-ial**	**-able**	**-ible**
_____	_____	_____	_____
_____	_____	_____	_____
_____	_____	_____	_____
_____	_____	_____	_____

Spelling Practice 10: Commonly Misspelled Words

Many words that are frequently misspelled contain vowel pairs or unpronounced consonants. Often these words have no rules for spelling and must be learned and remembered.

A. Write each misspelled word with missing vowel correctly. Check your spelling in a dictionary.

1. lonliness _____
2. biscit _____
3. henous _____
4. efficent _____
5. patrotism _____
6. forfit _____
7. celestal _____
8. recrut _____
9. villin _____
10. garantee _____

11. suvenir _____
12. discret _____
13. parlament _____
14. luxurius _____
15. langush _____
16. prestege _____
17. capricous _____
18. chamis _____
19. sargent _____
20. outragous _____

B. Write the missing, unpronounced consonants in these words. Then, write two more words
with the same unpronounced letter. Use a dictionary, as necessary.

1. recei__t _____ _____
2. dis__ipline _____ _____
3. balle__ _____ _____
4. ya__ht _____ _____
5. __narled _____ _____
6. condem__ _____ _____
7. __sychology _____ _____
8. s__issors _____ _____
9. gram__ar _____ _____
10. id__ll _____ _____
11. dis__uade _____ _____
12. fer__et _____ _____
13. colon__ade _____ _____
14. re__nown _____ _____
15. __nome _____ _____
16. dis__ern _____ _____
17. whis__le _____ _____
18. rh__thm _____ _____
19. ex__ibit _____ _____
20. r__inoceros _____ _____